The Hanford Reach

Gregory McNamee, SERIES EDITOR

The Hanford Reach

A Land of Contrasts

TEXT BY Susan Zwinger

PHOTOGRAPHS BY Skip Smith

The University of Arizona Press   Tucson

The University of Arizona Press
Text © 2004 Susan Zwinger
Photographs © 2004 Stamford D. Smith
All rights reserved

♾ This book is printed on acid-free, archival-quality paper.
Manufactured in the United States of America

09 08 07 06 05 04 6 5 4 3 2 1

Library of Congress Cataloging-in-Publication Data appear on the last
printed page of this book.

contents

photographs

PHOTOGRAPHS

X

acknowledgments

So many people are part of this book. I want to thank Rex Buck and the Wanapum tribe for many hours spent on their ancestral land, Dr. Darby Stapp of Battelle Pacific Northwest National Laboratory for his knowledge of the cultural resources, and Heidi Newsome and Randy Hill of the U.S. Fish and Wildlife Service for their passion about birds, plants, and sagebrush ecosystems. The Whidbey and the North Cascades Institutes, along with their excellent workshop participants, grace these pages. Particularly helpful were Jeff Muse and Debi Martin, who arranged NCI logistics, and Bill Graves and Larry Deloz, who set up the Whidbey Institute field trips. Author Jack Nisbet added his vast knowledge of the east side, and Paul Patterson gave us a firsthand description of the radioactive waste cleanup.

I am indebted to my friends Frances Wood and Dorothy Read, and to the Sno-Isle Langley Library folks, Jamie Whitaker, Robin Obata, and Vicky Welfare. The Nature Conservancy of Washington has been outstanding in supplying experts and the most current plant lists. I also wish to thank Mike Ritter of the Hanford Reach National Monument and Pam Camp of the Bureau of Land Management in Wenatchee, as well as Brent Cundela for his expertise on the Missoula Ice Dam floods. Teri Peiper of the Moses Lake Audubon inspired me with her love of coulee geology. Thanks, too, to all east-side natural history lovers who added their insights to this book. I appreciate my excellent editors at The University of Arizona Press, Patti Hartmann and Greg McNamee.

ACKNOWLEDGMENTS

The Hanford Reach

introduction

A reach is one's fullest expansion, a dream, a goal, and a stretch toward our maximum potential. A reach is also that gesture of the human arm and soul we use to lean out toward one another. Over chasms of misunderstanding, even war, we reach out to comfort, to support, to understand, and eventually to love.

Reach, the noun, verb, and concept, takes up half a column in my unabridged dictionary. The "reach" in Hanford Reach means an expanse of river or sea between two natural boundaries, usually between two bends or bites. Here, the Reach is the last free stretch of the Columbia River between the McNary and the Priest Rapids dams. This book is about an open S curve of the Columbia River and the landscape forty miles on either side, from Vantage in central Washington to the Wallula Gap on the Oregon border. The Hanford Reach is a land of contrasts—lush green orchards against bleached floodplains, voluminous water and wetlands juxtaposed to desert soil, and the wild ecosystem surrounding nuclear reactors.

5:40 AM Lying on my side with no tent to screen me, I peer through the predawn light at the perforated, rust-colored rock before me. I arrived at midnight and fell to sleep on cold lava next to the Columbia River. Under the dim sky, I smell frosted plants and a damp aridity. The river reflects a salmon dawn sky, but where a slight breeze riffles the surface, waves reflect sage blue-green. Like silk threads on a loom, the two colors shift and shimmer. Closer in, my eye focuses on the deep purple of a delphinium. Larkspur! This asymmetrical bloom with its top sepal growing upward in a long tube has delighted me ever since my Colorado mountain childhood. The morning dawns clear in a land of wide river and tall cliffs. And it's not raining.

Drape a landscape over the knife's edge of the Cascades, drench the western half with Pacific storms, and scorch the other half with hot dry air, and you have the essence of the West in all its splendor and contrast. The Cascades and the Pacific Rim's Ring of Fire volcanoes have created a jarring juxtaposition—a desert in glaciated land. As a desert rat from the Southwest now living on a rainy west-side island, I must return to the desert periodically. Eastern Washington is dry shrub-steppe ecology complete with sand dunes. A finger of a Great Basin–like desert runs up the rain shadow east of the Cascades into British Columbia. As far north as Lillooet, British Columbia, I have found prickly pear, sagebrush, and chamisa, as if New Mexico had been toying with an out-of-body experience and lost part of itself.

Ecologists do not call the Hanford Reach a desert, but the leather-skinned, wind-beaten trappers and settlers who came after Lewis and Clark did. By their sheer fortitude and suffering, the pioneers have won the right to call it what they wish, and I follow suit. The rain shadow guarantees that much of the Reach has less than six inches of rainfall a year. It bakes in three-digit degrees in the summer and freezes your extremities in the winter. Wind howls up narrow gaps in the lava ridges, strong enough to drive settlers mad and kill cattle. The sun against thousand-foot black basalt cliffs bakes one's brains out. Throw in mean-looking grandfather rattlesnakes, scrawny prickly pear, desert varnish and canyon wrens, dehydration, windstorms and bare lithosols—I call this a desert.

The Hanford Reach is a landscape of irony. In 2000, President Clinton protected 560 square miles of south central Washington as the Hanford Reach National Monument, encouraging visits for research and education. The monument includes the Columbia's last free-flowing, nontidal stretch and the shrub-steppe ecosystem around it. The landscape owes its preservation to the Manhattan Project and the Cold War, which claimed thousands of acres in the early 1940s to build the world's first nuclear bombs.

By 1943 about fifteen hundred people lived in small towns

Basalt cliff with sand dune at base

along the river shore—White Bluffs, Ringold, Hanford, and Richland. Cattle grazed across what is now the Wahluke Unit, but not extensively. Its weather was too harsh—too much wind, too cold in winter, too hot in summer. Now Hanford is an ecological and cultural time capsule extremely valuable to scientists. Because Hanford has been off limits to the public since 1943, important archaeological resources that were destroyed elsewhere in the region have been preserved. The original shrub-steppe ecosystem has had sixty years to recover. The largest original tract of shrub-steppe in North America, it is a national treasure. The sagebrush, which dominates most of central Washington and the Great Basin desert, supports a complete ecosystem within its branches—symbiotic sage sparrows, sage grouse, sage thrashers, pygmy rabbits, sagebrush lizards, and many others.

Western Washington is famous for its rain forest, glaciers, abundant rivers, and persistent rain, while east of the Cascades, I can see for miles in every direction. My pineal gland is ecstatic. By day I explore the coulees and potholes scoured out of the lava flows. At night, with no cities nearby, I stare at multitudinous stars and give myself over to a world of night critters chortling, cooing, clucking, and howling their way across the mesas.

When Gregory McNamee asked me to write about Washington's arid lands for the *Desert Places* series, I offered to ride, walk, and paddle every inch of Hanford allowed. My perverse nature chose this arid region because it is unexpected and controversial.

My task is to celebrate the arid landscape. Even though the

radioactive cleanup is going more slowly than expected, we can revel in the ecosystem that the Cold War has saved. I could list statistics of radioactive elements that seeped into groundwater—thus into fish, cows, and people—that would melt down your hearts and minds, but other books better serve that purpose (for example, Michele Gerber's *On the Homefront: The Cold War Legacy*).

I've listened to the ranchers and farmers who have a long presence on the land; they know it as well as anybody. The relationship between the cow and sagebrush, between farm irrigation and wildlife, between man and untouched land exists in a tense balance. Time will heal some old wounds between the government, the military, the conservationists, and the residents. The families downwind from the plutonium production who have lost loved ones to high cancer rates have wounds that won't be healed.

I want to celebrate what is preserved in the horseshoe-shaped buffer zone seized in 1943 to protect Hanford's secrecy—Rattlesnake Mountain (Fitzner-Eberhardt ALE Reserve), Saddle Mountain, River Corridor, and Wahluke Arid Lands Ecology Reserve Units. Since these areas have become the Hanford Reach National Monument under a joint jurisdiction of the U.S. Fish and Wildlife Service and the Department of Energy, restoration has begun. Battelle's Pacific Northwest National Laboratory works with the Native people to protect cultural resources, such as sacred sites and the rituals still held on these lands. Thanks to the Nature Conservancy, the Bureau of Land Management, Fish and Wildlife, and university researchers, inventories of plants and animals have begun. Of the 725 vascular plants listed, two new plant species, a bladderpod and a buckwheat, have been named within the last few years. Forty-seven of these plants are species of concern. Insect species as yet unknown to man trundle through the sagebrush. Tens of thousands of birds rest and feed here on their way north or south. Since population growth along the West Coast has paved over many riparian areas, Hanford's become even more important.

This fall, I kayaked the Columbia through Hanford Reach with scientists and activists who are helping to restore it. Scary radioactive statistics aside, it is stirring country. We drifted with loons and cormorants, flirted with eddies, sought wild salmon redds, and were dwarfed by white cliffs.

The geology is grand. This desert is unique, sculpted by biblical-style floods carving sheet lava that exists nowhere else on the planet. As in all deserts, the bones of the earth are exposed. Time is transparent as layers of history and prehistory overlap in the dry air. Petroglyphs stand next to nuclear reactors—freeways next to ancient fishing platforms.

Hanford's present landscape began to form some sixty million years ago when successive lava layers poured over the land from giant cracks to the east in Idaho and near Ice Harbor Dam on the Snake River. Because the Pacific tectonic plate was subducting under the lighter continental plate, pressure built up in the earth, and melted rock rose. Basaltic sheets thousands of feet thick flowed for millions of years: the largest geologically recent lava event on earth.

Then came the ice.

Coulee created by floods near the end of the last ice age

During the four ice ages, the glacial lobes formed ice dams behind which water collected in vast Lake Missoula, covering all of northern Montana. When an ice dam broke, it sent a wall of water half a mile high pounding through central Washington at the rate of nine and a half cubic miles per minute. At fifty miles per hour, the force of the floodwater exerted thirty-three times the force of the greatest earthquake. The floods blasted down through solid basalt hundreds of feet thick, creating strange landforms unique in the West. Whirlpools scoured out potholes, called colbs, and vertical dry waterfalls, the tallest of which were a thousand feet high. An unusual landform, the coulee—from the French *couler*, meaning "to flow"—were eerie, vertical-walled canyons carved not by river time but by sheer force. Archaeological evidence suggests that Native Americans were already here when the last dam broke, around twelve thousand years ago. I try to imagine what a prehistoric family felt, hearing the great roar of the air mass pushed in front of the wall of water.

Vast lakes collected over the Hanford Reach, lapping up against the mountains. As they dried out, they left a fine, white, powdery sediment full of diatoms and other life. The eight-hundred-foot-tall White Bluffs along the Columbia are old lake-bottom layers interspersed with ash from various volcanoes.

Beginning in the 1930s, the American government built huge dams, such as the Grand Coulee, which in turn filled quirky-shaped lakes in the squiggle-shaped colbs and smaller coulees nearby. Just as Lake Powell covers over the magnificent red-pinnacled sandstone of Glen Canyon, this phenomenon creates vertical canyon walls that plunge uncannily down into dark waters. We humans expect gentle edges to our lakes, seamless mergers of land and water on which one can lie and lunch and dream. Not in the potholes and flooded coulees.

Today is a critical time for the deserts of Washington. As the last patches of original shrub-steppe disappeared across the West under industrial farming, housing developments, and off-road vehicles, the Hanford Reach has been able to preserve large tracts. Scientists have just begun to unfold the land's treasures—an ecosystem time capsule, petroglyphs, ancient village sites, new species, geological wonders.

As I drive along the floodplain of the river, a seventy-foot-high dust devil spins out of a dry field. Just for kicks, I drive through it. Adrenaline zings out to my feet and fingers as the wind knocks my pickup sideways. Some desert tribes once believed that whirlwinds are the preferred mode of transport for powerful shamans. In its vortex, I can almost hear the shaman inside warning me to honor the land.

for the love of lava

Rain splatters in high winds. Waves wrinkle the expanse of the Columbia. I camp south of Vantage on a mounded lava flow called the Roza. Highway 243 is a diminutive drama of a road that clings to the Columbia River as it saws its way through ridge after ridge of folded basalt. In a wetter piece of the world, this stone would be covered with forest.

Although basalt is not a pretty rock, I have come to love all the varied lava characters. Each is unique in chemical composition, in cooling time, in fracture joints. Each has a name, a birth date, and a particular ecosystem on top. Some are a jaunt on Mars, others a stroll through exquisite rock gardens. Some are so perfectly cubistic that Marcel DuChamp's *Nude* could have descended in style. Another has tall, thin columns in metallic hues with chartreuse lichen. Some columns waver sideways. Others turn completely on their sides so that their tops are turned toward us, a parquet floor of hexagons.

Some basalts sandwich thick layers of brick-red soil, baked as the next lava flow covered it. Others reveal white lenses of old lake bottoms or thirteen-thousand-year-old Mount Saint Helen's ash.

Some basalts shine like obsidian. Others weather into bright rusts and greens. Sheet basalt flows out as viscous liquid, because it contains little steam or silicate to explode. The more silicate, the more lava exudes in the light pastels of dactite or rhyolite, a crumbling rock that can erode into strange spires and tent shapes. The most explosive creates volcanic ash as light as snow.

My favorite lava, the Roza, sharp and nasty to walk on, is a stunning rock garden in spring, covered with pointillistic mounds of flowers. This pulvinate (shaped like a pincushion, to preserve moisture) cosmos is blotched in saturated golds, purples, whites, and pinks March through June. Some, like the Carey's balsamroot, are extroverts, big and brassy. The variety of buckwheats, the *Eriogonum*, strike in subtle chords of pastels. Thyme-leafed buckwheat is a little mosaic treasure box, while rock buckwheat blooms in gold balls.

On the Roza flow I hover two hundred feet above the wide Columbia River. The sky is storm-dark except for the Vantage Bridge catching sun like a long, neon cat's cradle. To the south

Columnar basalt: Tall basalt columns provide resting sites for birds as is evidenced by accumulations of "whitewash" or guano.

the Wanapum Dam releases a vast thunder of water. Its spray rises four hundred feet, its mists are full of rainbows. Below on steely water four loon species converge: Pacific, common, yellow-billed, and red-throated loon—an unusual combination, a sign of how important this flyway is for migrating birds. The surface of the dam-swollen river is covered with wide, troubled eddies—an inverted van Gogh *Starry Night.* Eddies are signs of water backfilling over the cliffs and spires of a natural canyon. Before the Wanapum Dam drowned the Wanapum tribal homeland in 1958, this ancestral fishing place marked the end of a long series of mighty river rapids. Two dams generate power within eighteen miles of each other, because the river drops 230 feet between Vantage and Priest Rapids. With this volume of water, these rapids once rivaled the Colorado River in the Grand Canyon. Here, the Wanapum sat on their traditional fishing platforms and scooped out salmon one after another. Now no Wanapum can support a family or make a living from wild fish.

After the Roza lava, I drive to the tiny town of Beverly, where the river sliced through thousand-foot lava walls. Just south of Beverly, a delicate railroad bridge, begun in 1907 and abandoned in the 1970s, tethers Sentinel Gap together. The small highway hairpins around the cliff on a cut in sheer rock, while a delivery truck barrels down from behind me, ignoring the thirty-five-miles-per-hour limit. I barely have time to glance at the long, white lenticular sediment high in the cliff. The Beverly Formation settled from quiet lake waters that deposited millions of microscopic diatoms. Ironically, it was these very animals who would donate their bodies for cement to build the Wanapum and Priest Rapids dams fourteen million years later.

Basalt cliff and clouds near Beverly

I pull over in a narrow lava gap where one enticing, pale sand dune leans up against dark columns. Wind speeds up through the gap, then slows down and drops loess particles in an ivory-colored silk scarf up the cliff. This singular dune has always drawn me to it. Today will hit ninety degrees, but at 6:30 AM, I shiver on the dune top in the shadow of Grande Ronde lava. Great continental glaciers sheered off its pearly sand from the bedrock. Long, angular loess particles will stack high but will not sing, as rounded quartz sand dunes will. Twelve years ago I tried to start loess sand "singing" in dunes on the east side of Hanford by plunging down steep, bare, sand faces. All I got was sand stuck to sweaty places. Now protected as wilderness by the Bureau of Land Management, a gush of desert life stabilizes those dunes. Sooner or later sand dunes all over the region will disappear, since the river no longer floods, no longer deposits raw dune material—sand.

From my high perch, I spy the birds-of-prey overlooks on the top of octagonal columns. The long drips of white guano through the orange and chartreuse lichens are handsome against the dark stone. Prairie falcons, peregrines, and kestrel perch here, keeping a sharp eye out for rodents whose prolific tracks crisscross the dune.

Suddenly a spiral trill of familiar hosannas. I so miss this ultimate songster of the desert Southwest, but here he is—a Washingtonian canyon wren!

Enjoying the cold, I remain a long time writing. Soon the sun will sear the Grande Ronde, as jagged as giant saw teeth. I kneel, examining the frilled can-can skirts of evening primroses.

Wind-whipped grasses etch arcs in the sand. Steep-angled shadows cast each plant with an elongated purple copy.

The break between the lower lava flow and the tall columns on top marks the Vantage interbed, a 15.6-million-year-old sediment, which holds entire ginkgo trees preserved to their cellular level. Travelers over I-90 pull off in Vantage on the Columbia River to ogle at ancient tree rings and petroglyphs at Ginkgo State Park. South down the Columbia, catastrophic flooding signs are abundant: giant ripples, cobble flood bars a hundred feet high, truck-sized boulders, sediment smeared high up the cliffs. I am held in a gentle land of past violence—vast lava sheets and half-mile-high roaring torrents.

Sun spears shoot down through each V-crevice in the rocky maw behind me, stabbing my back with heat. Picking up some thirty empty beer bottles marring the sand, I drive south through the ten-million-year-old Elephant Mountain flow, which tilts steeply and mimics pachyderm skin. Across the river the immense Umtanum Ridge layers stand up vertically and eroded to points, looking like a row of old-fashioned clothes irons. In between, soft gray-green carpets pour down over the irons at steep angles of repose, talus covered with vegetation. These anticlinal ridges, which so define south central Washington, have scrambled all the previous volcanic and flood features.

My time-limited human mind fails to grasp how the ancestral Columbia River carved so many routes, shoved about like a toy train track. It once looped far west toward the rising Cascades and flowed through the present town of Yakima, before ridges rose and the river contorted in a big bend around Hanford.

Time for a plate tectonics demonstration. Lay out a big bath towel, running north-south to represent the sheets of lava that heaved out of cracks in the ground. Now pretend that you are the Pacific tectonic plate, and flop down on your belly on the west side of the towel (your feet hit the San Andreas fault, your fingers tickle Canada). Inch your way north along the towel using your toes. Large wrinkles should be forming in the towel. These wrinkles, called the Olympic–Walla Walla Lineament, align east-west and pile up all the way from Oregon to the northeast corner of the Olympic Peninsula.

Now stand up and gaze south-southeast past the Umtanum Ridge. There, on the south side of Hanford, lies the largest wrinkle, Rattlesnake Mountain. At 3,666 feet, it rises 644 feet higher than Snoqualmie Pass over the Cascade Mountain Crest.

The Columbia arches around some ridges and cuts down through others. Contorting around the Rattlesnake and Yakima ridges, the river saws through Saddle Mountain and the Umtanum. Thirty miles south of the Tri-Cities the Columbia loops around to the west and creates the Wallula Gap by cutting through the Horse Heaven Hills, leaving the Two Sisters, two lava pinnacles.

As I drive south, the Umtanum Ridge forces the Columbia to take a right angle turn to the east. I feel dwarfed below two thousand feet of upturned lava flows. Now the layers upend, now they bend over backward. The black rock looks molten, wavering in the heat. Taking fifteen million years to arch upward, this anticlinal ridge broke at the top, so that the Pomona basalt at two thousand feet is also on the bottom of the river. I travel over giant river cobble and erratic boulders from the Missoula floods. Tamed, imprisoned water gives way to the last wild stretch of river after Priest Rapids Dam. Named for a Wanapum medicine man, not a Catholic leader, this dam was the brainstorm of Judge Cornelius Hanford. He saw a business opportunity and dammed the rapids, developing an extensive irrigation system for the town of Hanford.

Ah, the dams, the dams. Death to wild salmon and natural river flow but life to our contemporary electric economy. From the Roza lava to Priest Rapids, I have been traveling through an agricultural desert. Unlike other Western deserts, southeastern Washington thrives with that scarcest, life-giving commodity, water. Neat rows of orchards and vineyards flicker by in their stroboscopic rows, jarring green in the dry land. If it were not for this gracious river, this land would look much like the Nevada desert.

From dams come power lines. Power lines proliferate everywhere—from Hanford, over to Seattle, down to California. We are all fused in one great umbilical grid. The 2002 California power debacle brought death to more of our salmon by lowering the water levels here on the Columbia. The federal government ruled that we had to send our power to the sun bunny state.

High tension towers take on anthropomorphic shapes. Atop their metal legs, giant hexagonal hoops appear face-like, and the two springs in a V become angry eyebrows. The springs hold onto a central high-tension line, earthquake-proof—or so we suppose. Two sharp-angled shoulders end in two short arms, which fist two more power lines on either side like a vigilante holding two rifles.

Eerily, they remind me of Yei gods or ancient anthropomorphs etched in rock in the desert Southwest. Forgive me, Navajo and Zuni readers. Such a sacrilegious comparison might be justified after all; electricity is the all-powerful deity of our era.

After Priest Rapids, the Columbia turns east and begins the last remaining free-flowing stretch of this magnificent river. I follow it toward an intense wildflower display in the wild shrub-steppe ecosystem. I began this trip through an industrialized desert so that, in comparison, I might understand what we inadvertently saved.

forbidden fruit

Pale phlox blooms glow in the dark and hover two feet above the ground like squadrons of tiny spaceships. I rub my sleepy eyes and shake my head. Having slept near Othello, I entered the Wahluke as soon as it was legal, one hour before dawn under an overcast sky. Longleaf phlox is symbiotic with the sagebrush, growing not only under it, but up and through it. At this hour, the sage are shadows, but the phlox glows disembodied.

So begins the Wahluke, strange and lush, full of surprise. Ever since I craned my neck upward from a kayaker's perspective on the Columbia, I have wanted to perch on top of the White Bluffs. I pull onto a gorgeous overlook 730 feet above the river. The carvings of the ancient sculptor emerge slowly with the orange penumbra of dawn—sandbars, loops, cutoffs, sand dunes, cliffs, sloughs, and islands.

The landscape is so beautifully composed, it is as if Frederic Church, the Hudson River School landscape painter, carefully painted this scene, using the smooth, pale blue of the river to lend the eye rest and to frame the riotous hills. As in his landscapes, every element is perfectly composed for balance and pleasure. He often included only one small human figure out on an overlook, for proportion. With a brush laden with lavender blue, he splashed hills with waist-high lupines. He dabbed on yellow fiddlenecks. Here and there he painted ivory blobs where blocks of the pale cliff have fallen and lie disintegrating in bright mounds.

Far below, at least fifteen species of waterfowl and shorebirds are quacking and chortling. All around, meadowlarks, sage sparrows, and loggerhead shrikes chip-chip in the bushes. Raucous geese call high overhead. A Swainson's hawk and two ravens make lazy spirals climbing the updrafts. To the north beyond Saddle Mountain in Crab Creek, fifteen thousand sandhill cranes once danced in a field of unharvested corn. To the south I see another flock of cranes, gigantic devices for dismantling nuclear reactors down to their cores, leaning in Tinkertoy angles.

My eyes feast on the forbidden landscape of Hanford Nuclear Reservation. Across the river, the gigantic N Reactor rises from the flattest, lowest ground in the Pasco Basin. N Reactor was built in a resurgence of nuclear power during President Eisenhower's Atoms for Peace initiative. The first dual-purpose

Seeds: Fires are common in this region, but windblown seeds initiate new growth quickly.

reactor, it operated from 1963 through 1988 to produce plutonium for bombs and steam to generate electricity. From 1966
through 1987, N 105 and Bonneville Power Authority's adjacent
power plant were the largest producers of electricity in the country. Swords *and* plowshares—or in our case, swords and dish-
washers, aluminum, and airplane factories.

I struggle toward hope from our legacy of nuclear destruction as a Benedictine nun must struggle to feel love from a voice
she will never hear and a face she will not see. Gazing down on
the lushness of an original shrub-steppe ecology generates a faith
in the life force that will push forward long after we are gone.
Grand hundred-mile views mimic the trick of geologists and
novitiates: a switch in time scale from the "small I" to geologic
time. The endless arguments between the U.S. Department of
Energy, Washington State's Department of Ecology, the Tri-
Cities loyalists, and the environmentalists melt away. The hard
job of cleanup continues, inventing, stumbling, halting, hos-
ing, hefting, burying, and transporting us forward into a new
realm of consciousness.

The Ringold River Road, which runs through the River
Corridor Unit of twenty-five thousand acres, has long been
closed off, so I pull on boots. Nearby grows a plant unknown
to humans until a few years ago, a White Bluff bladderpod, as
well as two endemics, Geyer's milkvetch and desert dodder. I
hope to find them. At first my head is even with the top layers
of Ringold lake sediment, then it sinks into time. Horizontal
layers rise, some fine, some rough conglomerates. The Ringold
Formation came into being when lake sediment from the massive

Evening primrose on sand dune

Missoula Floods backed up water across the entire Pasco Basin. Startling white, hard layers represent ash from the Mt. Saint Helens and Mazama volcanoes. Each layer speaks of events that lasted centuries: fine loess silt denotes quiet waters. Huge, rough cobbles indicate flash floods, and even larger rock from Canada dropped as icebergs melted.

A solitary rock wren flies from outcrop to outcrop, always twenty feet ahead of me and singing loudly. Cliff swallows whir from shrub up to tiny holes in the cliff, carrying wriggling goodies. Two hundred feet lower, I drop over the road edge into the deeply eroding hillocks, thick as cross waves in a stormy sea.

The vegetation here is completely, astoundingly different from what is outside the Arid Lands Ecology Reserve. We've all heard about the original shrub-steppe, but I've never actually experienced it, never known the beauty of its palette and the variety of its forms. The hills are rusty red dotted with bluish sage. The native grasses grow tall and swirl in the breeze like silky human hair. Throughout are scattered the deep yellows of Cusick's sunflowers. The salsify, a showy ray flower with nine long green bracts protruding from the backs of thirteen gold petals, comes up to my thighs.

The whole scene is so lush with life, birds thick in the air, birds thick in the bushes, birds thick down on the water, that I am staggered. Above, on surrounding lands, the impact of the cow hoof has been greater. Here, grasses are so thick it is hard to walk through them. There is no place bare of vegetation to put my foot, and the ground is so uneven and unseen that it is hard to retain balance. I follow a deer trail that scallops along erosion gullies and climbs up an eighty-foot hummock of a hard ash layer.

Squatting on the cliff edge, I discover that I am sitting on top of a burrow big enough for a wolf, on its thin top of cemented ash. A coyote scat, full of red sticks, acts as a nameplate above her doorbell—had she a doorbell. Two hundred feet below me, the river cuts a vertical white cliff with an outer swing of swift current. I follow the hummock top trail with steep drop-offs to either side, then drop back down to the ground.

The earth is a rich, dark brown and black; its textured humps remind me of a prickly doormat over a pile of goose eggs. This is the healthiest cryptobiotic soil I have ever met. Centuries of minute filaments of cyanobacteria, fungus, algae, mosses, lichen, and tiny liverworts grow through the dry desert dirt until it rises like hardened cumulus on every inch of ground. Judging from its jet black globules, it probably contains gelatinous lichen, *Collema coccophorum,* very important because its cyanobacteria fixes nitrogen in the soil. I have no choice but to put feet on it, yet unlike in cattle country, it does not disintegrate into dust when stepped on. Overgrazing and grazing at the wrong time of year allows cows to make pastures into sidewalks. Mule deer and elk do graze here, but their eating pattern moves them lightly and seasonally over the land before they damage any one area.

Cryptobiotic soil deserves stardom and drumrolls in spite of its lowly nature. A living mulch, it retains moisture, squelches weed growth, reduces wind and water erosion, and builds organic matter in the soil for higher plants. Together these tiny plants form a matrix that binds the soil together and occupies nutrient-poor zones in arid lands where even angels fear to tread.

I climb back up to the road and continue south toward the Hanford village site. A spring and a thick, shady grove of ash and black cottonwood brought early settlers. These venerable old trees drape their branches down to the ground, and I crawl inside to lean against a trunk five feet in diameter. The tree room is thick with feathers and dung—many animals shelter from the heat in here. Outside it is eighty degrees, inside only sixty-eight. Magpies outside feeding their young ones are making a gleeful racket. River muck hangs ten feet high in the branches from the Columbia's wilder moments. I troop down to the river and plunge my bandanna in, then my whole head. On the river a lone Wanapum elder, a fishing line trailing, stands in his aluminum skiff. I know him as native because of his long braid and the fact that he has stood motionless like that for more than eleven thousand years.

No signs of the ash grove settlers remains. Only sixty years. How quickly we fade.

Across the road a steep deer trail angles up the white cliffs. At three hundred feet up, I crouch below an outcrop to feast my eyes. Below me sweeps a slope of bunchgrass, blue sage, and orange to brick-red hopsage. Even the reactors shimmer adobe pink in the diffused light.

Gazing west through the heat and the mauve grasses, I gulp with pleasure. Hundreds of giant purple sagebrush lilies bob in the breeze. I have never seen this sego lily before, in all my years in the West. Sheep and cattle eat it immediately. The sixteen-inch-

THE
HANFORD REACH

30

Dead tree at sunset, the Wahluke Unit, temperature 95°

tall plants seem impossible in this jagged place. Backlit by the sun, they are translucent like stained glass windows. The grasses are alive with flying beings: seedpods, butterflies, grasshoppers, and a flying antlike creature all black with red-orange wings and thorax. Also backlit, thousands of enormous, gossamer spiderwebs shine white in the sun.

Having pushed for most of a day through tall grasses, I return to the overlook to find my socks are embedded beyond repair with seed. What beauty I have earned—all for the price of a pair of socks.

On the drive out of the Wahluke, the journey takes a macabre turn. I take a right turn to find Lake Wahluke, then a wrong turn. An arrow-straight dirt track runs due north, then abruptly makes two right-angle turns into empty sagebrush, and terminates in what appears to be the end of civilization in a B movie. House foundations, driveways, metal signs with their burden of non sequiturs, but nothing else. No houses, no rusting trikes, no hints of gardens. Just wind shoving stale ghosts around.

the mighty chiawana

Adouble-crested cormorant flies upriver on fast wing beats, looking quite ancient, as if its ancestral phalacrocorays had just arrived from the Oligocene. We've seen many today. They love the cool, clear weather after a cold front passes. One yellow-faced bird lands so close to me that I can examine his powerful hind limbs and large feet for swimming. This double-crested fellow, unlike other cormorants, is maneuverable enough in flight that it can land in trees. They decorate pilings and snags like black crosses, wings held out horizontally to dry.

We thirty-odd folks from the Whidbey Institute arrived in the early morning, cliff swallows swishing near our heads, and thought of the generations of Sahaptian speakers.

Before launching our kayaks into clear waters under the Vernita Bridge this morning, we stood in a silent circle to consider the thousands of years this river has sustained the many tribes who lived on its shores. We watch for their messages chipped into cliffs, enigmatic geometric symbols invoking the gods or marking life's major passages. They also pecked bighorn sheep, which once roamed here. Their children sought guardian spirits along the river, where large trees floated from faraway forests to supply canoes and fuel. They dug freshwater mussels and caught eels. The river's reeds supplied mats for their houses.

In other words, *Chiawana*, meaning "great river" in the Wanapum language, is the giver of life, the river of myth, the caretaker. Coyote created the river for the Wanapum people, who were his charges. The spirit of the river is still honored in clandestine rituals. The Cayuse, Palouse, Nez Perce, Umatilla, Walla Walla, Yakama, and Wanapum mourn the loss of tens of thousands of acres of land not merely because they are deprived of real estate, but because they have lost part of themselves—their culture, heritage, and religion. The Columbia also brought traders, trappers, settlers, ranchers, and atomic scientists. It brought DuPont engineers and army generals, and Nike missiles. The rich volcanic ash soil on its banks brought farmers, who in turn brought ships, railroads, highways, and power lines. Now it brings kayakers and naturalists. One of us, Paul Patterson, works on the Superfund cleanup of nuclear radiation. We are authors, artists, lawyers, and parents. We float in silence, staring up at the stark Hanford nuclear facility on one side and a

Native American petroglyphs on basalt along the Columbia River

wild Saddle Mountain refuge on the other. We feel as if our brains are split in half, which, come to think of it, they are.

A sturgeon breaches. Early October and time for the giant chinook, or king, salmon to return to spawn in the Hanford Reach, last natural stretch of the Columbia. I watch for a fifty-pound salmon under my kayak. Even grander and stronger salmon once swam all the way up into the upland rivers of Canada, but the Grand Coulee Dam cut off thousands of square miles of habitat for them. Resting our paddles across our bows and not speaking, we hear the wings of scaups and buffleheads. On the north shore, rabbitbrush blooms yellow, while on the south, radioactive berry bushes have been yanked from the riverbank, leaving holes. In spring, long-billed curlews careened in for landings with their cinnamon underwings and seven-inch bills. Eagles, grebes, pintails, and goldeneyes will overwinter on Saddle Mountain Lake. To the south, tall gray concrete reactors loom nearby.

We pass many islands with complex channels never dammed or dredged—excellent fish habitat. A wild river has gravel bars, safety for molting birds, gravel bottoms for redds, oxbow ponds, riffles, backwater sloughs. In this fifty-one-mile free reach, 80 percent of the fall chinook and forty-three other fish species find shelter.

By mid-morning we stop for a lecture on past settlements, and in just forty minutes we find our kayaks high and dry. The McNary Dam is pouring water out from under us. Our voracious need for electricity is made tangible as we pick up the boats and lug them back to the water. Gone are the small rapids, the

Fishing platform: Members of the Yakama Nation still fish the waters of the Yakima River adjacent to the Hanford Reservation with traditional methods.

whirlpools, and the clean cobble shores. I worry about the salmon redds. Throughout the day, the water level continues to drop. Even the mergansers and grebes seem scarcer.

By 1:30, past when I have moved from hungry into dizzy, we pull in for lunch before the massive white cliffs. Their nine-hundred-foot loft startles us, as if we are in canyon country of the Colorado Plateau. Around us wander peccary, rhinoceros, woolly mammoth, camel, early horses, and even a panda—although we have missed them by two to ten million years. Out of the Ringold layers from the late Pliocene to early Pleistocene stepped giant otter, llamas, and sloths wearing only a few bones and their teeth. These early browsers and aquatic mammals lived in warm, humid swamps. By the late Pliocene, the ancient Cascades had risen enough to block off some of the moisture from the Pacific, and the larger fauna began to die out.

I marvel that this arid country could have been the confluence of three major ecozones: boreal forests and tundra, western woodlands, and bog. Such a convergence is evident in the extraordinarily complex pollen types. Layers of richness are hidden under a sea of sage. We float past two reactor sites where, Paul tells us, they are burying radioactive wastes, attempting to keep them out of the groundwater, and carefully resculpting the earth above to mimic nature. The Superfund workers have removed all the extra equipment, painted what is left in earth tones, and are tearing down all but the radioactive cores. These they will cover in concrete until they have built huge mounds. Yet all such protective measures may leak in a hundred years or so, and our grandchildren will have an expensive problem. Various measures to dispose of the waste on site have been researched, but most are based on the assumption that the ground around Pasco Basin does not move. Evidence to the contrary exists in the displacement of parts of Rattlesnake and Umtanum ridges. When workers bored holes throughout the Wanapum's sacred Gable Mountain, they found it riddled with fault lines.

Across the river, near reactors N and B, an eerie movement unfolded during the nineteenth and early twentieth centuries: the Ghost Dance. Tribes up and down the river believed an Armageddon would cleanse the land of its abusers, that the earth would heave up and the ancestors would rise again. The Plateau people believed that the world had always existed and would continue forever—that is, until European diseases arrived. Dry snow—volcanic ash—rained down to convince their prophets that a supernatural Chief, with Coyote's assistance, foreshadowed the world's end. The prophets told them to dance to hasten the apocalypse so that happier times would quickly follow. The Ghost Dance anticipated something terrible unfolding here, perhaps a prescience of nuclear weapons.

After lunch, we slide our kayaks into a muddy turbulence and skirt the cliffs. Loosely consolidated sediment ripples by in tan and pink and ivory layers. On top of them lies the Wahluke Unit. We float past Block Island, essential salmon spawning ground, and find huge white birds floating ahead—pelican-shaped soup tureens. Each summer these synchronistic fliers grace our rivers and lakes in eastern Washington and Oregon.

Just as the wind whips up, we round the bend to an opening in White Bluffs. A stream flows out, bringing sweet, clear water over oval cobble. I wait until it is my turn to ram my kayak up a mudflat toward what earlier today was shore. Two by two, we portage each boat up the steep, cobble bank to a gravel parking lot, the historic White Bluffs ferry landing.

Rows of ornamental trees shade a street that no longer exists. The major crossing for a century before modern railroads were built, the White Bluffs landing was essential for nineteenth-century commerce arriving upriver from the Pacific and crossing northward to supply miners in British Columbia and ranching communities throughout the Northwest.

Nothing is left of the busy dock. A 1910 photograph shows two ferries in dock, the *Kennewick,* with large portals for wagons, horses, and cargo, and a smaller ferry, its three decks crammed with more than sixty people. Women in long white dresses add a gala air. One can breathe in the exuberance of this new era of boom and growth and radical new technologies.

The town of White Bluffs planned to be an impressive center of commerce. "Rierson's Mercantile, 1918" shows wide storefronts with a draft horse and haul wagon in front. A photograph of an ice cream parlor, circa 1920, saddens me. The camera is close enough to show the faces of four townfolk standing in front of Beldin's Ice Cream and "Cigars and Tobacco" windows. Their familiar fancies and vices endear them to me. The faces are almost recognizable and shine with hopeful, hard-working character. I know that in twenty-three years they will receive terse government notices to evacuate. They will stand in lines or mill around in a large metal building holding government checks, looking lost and bewildered. The history of the Hanford

Nuclear Facility is about to commence, while their history ends.

Under the shade of their grand old trees, I watch the same warbling vireo, orange-crowned warbler, and goldfinch they must have. In low "quonks," ravens chortle and creak their raven love. I hear the long skirts of women swishing past.

looking for truth in all the dry places

Franklin Delano Roosevelt authorized the Manhattan Project in October 1939 to beat Hitler and Nazi Germany to the creation of an atomic bomb. Three top-secret atomic cities were selected: Los Alamos, New Mexico; Oak Ridge, Tennessee; and Richland, Washington. The military and the DuPont Corporation's engineers were to construct several nuclear reactors, chemical separation facilities, and fuel management facilities in order to produce sufficient amounts of plutonium for the world's first nuclear bombs.

December 7, 1941, Japanese planes bombed Pearl Harbor, drawing America into a world war. The rapid militarization of the United States accelerated its sudden rise to superpower and quickened the development of the atomic bombs. The plutonium for the Fat Man bomb originated here in the graphite reactors of Hanford.

Roosevelt put General Leslie Groves, whose office was in New York, in charge of the highly secretive project. Even though he had a three-man advisory board, he seldom consulted them. Acting unilaterally, he decided to abandon normal, orderly methods in the production. Design and production had to unfold as fast as possible, all based on meager laboratory experimentation. Safety was far less a concern than time.

One pleasant day in December 1942, Colonel Franklin Matthias walked with two DuPont Corporation engineers, gazing at the river, feeling the dusty soil, hearing the high "kerl" of a red-tailed hawk. They saw an empty wasteland, which was exactly what they wanted. When they visited what they saw as the dilapidated towns along the river, they did not talk to the locals. They were scouting for a home for the highly secretive military project needed to win World War II.

As Matthias and the DuPont engineers explored the tract, they discovered gravel, shale, and sandstone underlain by solid basalt. They needed immense amounts of power, water, isolation, and building materials. Of all the choices across the West, Hanford had it all. Only fifteen hundred people had to be removed from their homes, some with as little as thirty days' notice. The Manhattan Project required an isolated site in the West. Because of safety and security concerns, the site could not be near a coast. An exceptional amount of power would be available when the Grand Coulee and Bonneville dams ran their power lines right through Hanford. The Manhattan Project would need 25,000 gallons of water per minute to cool the reactors. It would need a flat land at least sixteen miles across. Locals could supply coal, oil, sand, and aggregate.

Matthias and the engineers did not see, or did not want to see, a thriving desert flora—sagebrush, ryegrass, rabbitbrush, bitterbrush, bluegrass, salt grass, bunchgrass, several kinds of buckwheat, prickly pear, willow, and sagebrush lilies. They did not see, or did not want to see, a complex substrata cut into a web of aquifers, cracks, springs, and faults. Matthias did not get down on the ground to identify a delicate milkvetch and bitterroot or surprise himself with the sight of a pygmy rabbit hopping by. He had a top-secret mission to complete.

By February 1943, the federal government seized 625 square miles of the Columbia River Basin for the Hanford Engineer Works under the War Powers Act. They offered the people living between Priest Rapids and Richland a meager compensation as they were ordered out of their homes and off their property. The government viewed the Hanford site as a wasteland isolated from population centers, which could be used at will for any national defense or resource extraction purpose, even extremely dangerous ones.

Land acquisition became a bitter controversy between the government and the landowners, a bitterness that lasts to this day. Before the land around Hanford Reach was protected as Arid Lands Ecology study areas under the jurisdiction of the Fish and Wildlife Service and the Department of Energy in 2000, some of the survivors and their offspring expected their land to be given back to them.

An entire production force moved into the industrial town of Richland within the year. Workers rapidly constructed the plutonium reactors, B, D, and F, spacing them a mile from one another. Plants T, U, and B were separated from one another by a mile and from the reactors by at least four miles. This ensured that an accident in any one area would not affect the operation of the other units. Today, that wide separation adds to a sense of emptiness of the Reach.

Workers began construction in March 1943 and completed most of it by April 1945. More than 780,000 cubic yards of concrete, steel, and cement blocks, 386 miles of highway, and housing for five thousand women and twenty-four thousand men all sprang up out of the desert. The men moved 25 million cubic yards of earth.

Securing construction design, such as checking future leaks, was very difficult, because speed was of the utmost necessity. Only small design variations were permitted to adapt to the actual site. To the workers' credit, all the buildings were completed on schedule with no major design flaws.

The workers were extremely patriotic. With their own paychecks, they bought a $162,000 B-17 bomber for the Air Corps. When it arrived from Boeing field in Seattle in July 1944, the celebration was the most effective morale builder during the Hanford nuclear development period. To this day, residents of the Tri-Cities are fiercely proud of their contribution to world security.

A quick lesson in plutonium production is impossible but necessary here. Area 300 was the initial stage in plutonium production. In 300, the nuclear fuel from metallic uranium took the form of pipe-shaped cylinders, or fuel slugs, which were then encapsulated in aluminum or zirconium. The fuel rods then were shipped by rail to Area 100 for irradiation. These plants ran along the south shore of the Columbia because they needed huge quantities of water to dissipate the heat.

The massive B Reactor, the world's first nuclear reactor, was constructed and taken to criticality by September 1944, in less than a year's time. B produced the world's first fissionable material for the world's first atomic bomb, tested at the Trinity site in New Mexico in July 1945. The Area 200 sites were chemical separation plants, the third stage in production, where the plutonium was extracted and purified. Area 200 separated, isolated, stored, and shipped the plutonium.

Secrecy was absolutely essential since the Germans were in a neck-to-neck race with the United States to produce their own atomic bomb. Roosevelt had no doubt that Germany would use an atomic bomb to control the world. Security was tight, including background investigations of employees, security education, classified areas, documents, security safeguards, and emergency preparedness. Only a select group of very few men knew the whole scope of the Manhattan Project. Even Joint Chiefs of Staff and scientists were kept in the dark. Great risks were taken in the name of war.

Because of its secretiveness, the Manhattan Project generated a heightened sense of adventure. A leading physicist, John

Fence and No Trespassing sign, Hanford Reservation

Wheeler, saw Hanford as "a song that hasn't been sung properly." He and the other scientists felt they were pioneers, heroes, and adventurers.

However, it did create frustration among the workers and others who lived in proximity. A number of rumors flew, some of them humorous or outrageous. Hanford was a germ warfare factory, a camp for prisoners of war, a synthetics plant, a munitions factory, mines for valuable ore, a bombing range, the Roosevelts' summer home, or a lab for macabre human experiments. None could guess the true enormity of the Manhattan Project and its repercussions for the world.

The bombs dropped on Hiroshima and Nagasaki did end World War II but began the nuclear age. The chemistry necessary to extract plutonium from uranium creates millions of gallons of radioactive waste. Sixty million gallons are still stored in Hanford in 177 subsurface tanks in Area 200. One hundred forty-nine tanks were built with only a single carbon-steel shell in concrete and by 1964 had leaked at least one million gallons of radioactive liquid into the ground. The remaining twenty-eight double-shelled tanks appear not to have leaked—so far.

In the greatest incident of atmospheric contamination at Hanford, an experiment called the Green Run in December 1949 released almost eight thousand curies of Iodine-131 into the air in just two days. This radioiodine goes straight for human and animal thyroid tissue. The operation used raw uranium fuel slugs cooled in only sixteen days. Because the Soviet Union had detonated its first bomb, and in their rush had used the short-cooled fuel rods, the United States ran their own dangerous tests to measure radiation amounts. Green Run radiation was so powerful that it was detected at considerable distances around the globe. The resultant contamination of air and vegetation throughout large stretches of the Pacific Northwest were extremely high. Men in contamination suits and helmets would arrive without a word in residents' backyards, taking soil samples. The highest level, measured at Kennewick, was one thousand times the tolerable limit. Elevated cancer rates in the beautiful ranchland of the Palouse Hills in eastern Washington have been linked to this run. When a contemporary state health official was asked what he would do today in case of a Green Run, he said he would immediately evacuate all of eastern Washington, parts of Idaho, and northern Oregon.

Throughout the history of Hanford, the public has been reassured that the threat to human health was minimal. This, combined with the veil of total secrecy, lulled a trusting public. A pattern of ignoring public health concerns in the name of other necessities lasted throughout the Cold War until the mid-1980s. Then, in 1986, the excrement hit the cooling device.

When I lived in Santa Fe, New Mexico, only forty miles from Los Alamos, and had scientist friends who worked on nuclear "devices," I heard little of Hanford, much like the rest of the country outside of Washington and Oregon. As one of my editors remarked upon hearing my book title, "What's Hanford? A country club in Connecticut?" Yet I was morbidly fascinated with the Trinity site. The year I moved to Seattle, 1987, the Richland community wounds were raw. In February 1986, the Department of Energy, having taken over from the Atomic

Energy Commission, released nineteen thousand pages of documentation on the radioactive and chemical wastes released over the years. Indian Health Services and the governments of Washington and Oregon worked frantically with the United States Centers for Disease Control to calculate radiation doses for people living near Hanford. The Pacific Northwest suffered a communal shock and grief at the betrayal of scientists and the government. The Downwinders, ranchers and farmers living in a fan shape spreading north and east out of Hanford, saw cancer rates soar.

Richland was particularly bitter. Not only had the workers' families been exposed for years, but their sense of loyalty, patriotism, and immense pride in an almost impossible task well done, a scientific triumph, transformed overnight into shock. Some denied the truth of the documents. Others howled, "How could our government release such lethal waste and not inform us?" From the heady success in World War II they believed that science was infallible and the government never wrong.

I remember safety analyst Paul Patterson's firsthand narrative of the Superfund cleanup and feel encouraged. He explained how most areas will be returned to natural habitat. As Superfund cleanup workers remove buildings and rebury tanks, they will restack rock to look like natural ridges. One hundred forty-nine single-shelled tanks full of "nasty stuff" will be emptied, double-shelled, put back into the ground, and automatically monitored for leakage. Their radioactive contents will be vitrified on site and shelled in stainless steel. "Clean to Close" means filled with grout, buried, and guaranteed against leakage for a thousand years. From Paul's point of view, the process is going well. Of course, the State of Washington's ecology department and environmentalists do not agree.

Judges across the West are demanding higher standards of the Department of Energy. On July 2, 2003, District Judge B. Lynn Winmill in Boise ruled that the DOE uses illegal shortcuts in cleanup, because the Hanford tanks' former leakage is moving in a plume underground toward the groundwater, then the Columbia. This eventually moves up the food chain. Even as the Bush administration cuts back on the Superfund, I hold on to the hope that we as a people will have the political will to heal the land.

To cope with the cognitive dissonance Hanford causes, I think of an F. Scott Fitzgerald quote. He claimed that the sign of intelligence was to hold two or more conflicting ideas in your head at once. It is possible to acknowledge Hanford's part in Hitler's defeat, that the science accomplished in the Hanford Nuclear Facility was truly astonishing, *and* that we have launched a new era of environmental responsibility.

top of the world

Long braids fall below his waist across his checked work shirt. His wide, bronze face has features of a full-blood Sahaptian speaker of the Wanapum tribe. Dr. Darby Stapp, cultural resource specialist for Battelle's Pacific Northwest National Laboratory, introduces him as Rex Buck, spokesman for his tribe, to our North Cascades Institute group. Darby, a forty-something man dressed in khaki slacks, works with the Wanapum and other tribes for the protection of sacred areas and rituals. Rex has graciously agreed to meet us at the Vernita Bridge in front of his sacred mountain, Rattlesnake. He speaks:

"We use a *Shahápton* dialect, only fifty real speakers left in the world, and two hundred who speak somewhat. We have an oral history of the Great Flood, so our people have been here long before that time. We escaped up Rattlesnake Mountain when the waters came," he says, gesturing in back of him. "We had countless winter camps along this river all the way down to Pasco.

"We never had any laws. We did not need them. Now there's lots of intertribal politics. We never signed a treaty with the United States government like other tribes. We have no reservation but they built us houses along the river. We don't get a million dollars, like the Nez Perce, Umatilla, and Yakama tribes, because we signed no treaty. We didn't want to sign our land away.

"Before Hanford, we got along with the whites all right, with these farmers," Rex says, gesturing north toward the orchards. "We would pick their corn for them. We were OK until '43. The B Reactor was built on our sacred ground. Over there, you see our ancient road to Gable Mountain. We were peaceful, living in mat lodges beside the river until the fifties. Then the dams flooded our homeland and destroyed our fishing platforms at the bottom of rapids. There the salmon would leap up the falls, and we caught them by the hundreds."

Rex continues, showing no emotion, "Now we have no jobs, nothing to do. I have a government job in addition to working for the tribe. Gable Mountain's real name is Nook Shi, the Beaver, and is very sacred to the Wanapum. In order to store nuclear waste, the DOE drilled our sacred butte full of holes, only to find that it was unsuitable."

"This is a three-culture landscape," explains Darby Stapp.

"Native American, white, and Hanford. Ten thousand years ago, nomadic people followed larger game animals using the Clovis, then the Folsom, arrowheads. Then eight to four thousand years ago, the population exploded, and new kinds of animals and plants were added to the diet. We know this from finding bones and seeds with archaic tools in the middens. Today, Annabelle Rodriguez of the Department of Energy is in charge of balancing the needs of Indians with their own operations, because laws, such as the Indian Religious Freedom Act, require it. It's an almost impossible job, because the tribes are hesitant to reveal sensitive locations to the government."

Darby and Rex share a smile indicating a warm friendship. "The Wanapum are working hard to revitalize their ancient practices and beliefs."

"Even with no laws or lawyers, our tribes had a major trade for food and other valuables which stretched across the west. Many of your highways were native trails following the most direct routes," continues Rex. "Now with no jobs, nothing to do, alcoholism, diabetes, and a break in our religious traditions so involved with the salmon, our tribe is shrinking. We can no longer make our living by fishing. The great salmon runs are gone. The dams stop them."

Rattlesnake Mountain rises in back of Rex Buck like a holy monolith and fills the horizon. "We keep our rituals secret, but we have to warn the government when we will be going and where. A difficult thing, telling and not telling. But we don't want them to dump radioactive waste on us," he says with a sly grin.

The dirt track straight up Rattlesnake Mountain appears too steep for a car, but Heidi Newsome's Fish and Wildlife Carryall has no trouble. I have longed to reach the top of isolated Rattlesnake Mountain for years. Protected by the Atomic Energy Commission in 1967 as a buffer zone, the 120-square-mile Fitzner-Eberhardt ALE Reserve was named an ecological research area in 1972. Heidi looks just as I expect a ranger to look—sturdy, tanned, slim, light brown hair in a businesslike braid down her back. Heidi's job is to study and protect the Reach, as well as to educate the public.

Ascension is enlightening as we rise through ecozone after ecozone in eight miles. Lynn, Trevor, Martha, and Wayne, my North Cascades Institute students, make Heidi stretch out the drive to two hours by hopping out of the vehicle every thousand-foot gain in elevation. Heidi, who was "volunteered" for this task by her boss and at first seemed hesitant, succumbs to our enthusiasm—and charm. We envy her job.

At 1,100 feet, thousands of large sulfur lupine plants turn the mountainside lavender, with dashes of golden balsamroot and reddish purple fireweed. Farther up, we reach a band of yellow, an invasive tumble mustard. Even the lithosols, the thin rocky dirt over the basalt crust, is changing. We began in Warden silt loam, moved up to the Ritzville, full of volcanic ash. On the steepest slopes, the Kiona silt loam consists of dark gray basalt fragments. My favorite, the Lickskillet soil loam, dark brown and seemingly too shallow for plants, graces the very top of the ridges. Yet it is on the Lickskillet that we find the most unusual, dwarfed species.

Cracked basalt with lichens, moss, and grass, early stages of ecological succession on bare rock

At 1,210 feet Heidi shows us a sudden change in plant life, where ice age Lake Lewis reached its greatest height. We find it hard to imagine that any lakeshore reached this elevation. Upward Heidi drives, the old Carryall's engine roaring, nose pointing heavenward. Trevor spies brodiaea and yellow bell lilies, so Heidi stamps on the brakes—again. All four doors spring open, and we spring out. As we gain elevation, the earth spreads out below, more and more magnificent. Lynn points out an orange globe mallow.

Because the wind roars across the top of Rattlesnake Mountain, only plants evolved into pulvinate forms survive, their low domes cutting down on wind abrasion. At 2,240 feet I spy my first rosy balsamroot, rare, exquisite and indigenous to these high ridges. Prostrate along the Lickskillet lithosol, it blushes rosy orange with divided basal leaves, completely unlike its large, lowland cousin. A crouching milkvetch's lavender pea-flowers creep along the ground next to a salt and pepper lomatium.

Finally we reach the top of the world at 3,666 feet, with a view out over the entire Columbia Basin. Three cities tuck into the oxbows of the Columbia. I can make out the white Vs of Horn Rapids on the Yakima River, where the Wanapum still fish from wooden platforms built out over the current. The shining Columbia looks like a dimpled, stainless steel snake as it loops its lazy S curve east, then south, then back west through the Wallula Gap in the Horse Heaven Hills. Clear is the ancient track Wanapum feet have worn on the desert floor toward Nook Shi.

In the blue distance, the Missoula Ice Dam flood paths become clear to us. Water poured into the Pasco Basin from the north-west through the scoured and widened cliffs along the Columbia. Floods poured south from the Channeled Scablands near Othello, and flowed in from the northeast down the Esquatzel Coulee. Finally, we can envision wide Lake Lewis filling the entire basin like a small sea. Heidi explains a mysterious mile-long tube in the desert floor as a device to test the gravitational anomalies of the planet, a poetic concept to ponder. We could crouch here all day with Heidi, identifying plants, but the constant wind force chills us and changes our minds.

A month later, I return to Rattlesnake Mountain early in the morning. It is a different mountain. After last evening's hard rain, it radiates a warm mossy green, like the back of a velveteen family sofa. Low-angled shafts of sunlight poke through the clouds, spotlighting the plains. Cloud shadows roll across the Umtanum and Yakima ridges like sheep on wheels. Sun patches on the Columbia create silver puzzle pieces. After the fury of storm winds last night, this morning is perfectly still.

This time we enter the padlocked Fitzner-Eberhardt ALE Unit with members of the Whidbey Institute with special permission. Today we are able to see clear south to the Blue Mountains and John Day River country in Oregon. With a glow of cleanly washed vegetation, it is easy to understand how tribal members still visit this mountain on vision quests. We understand why our visits are limited—only the holiest of tribal shamans were once allowed up here. Vegetation is very fragile and easily trampled.

On foot we drop over the north edge of the top ridge down

to a spring on a steep slope. We wade through a meadow splashed with colorful hyacinth, death camas, bluebells, and forget-me-nots. A young horned lizard squats like a shrunken dinosaur on mud lumps. Frances, an excellent birder, spies a prairie falcon nest in the basalt cliff above us. Suddenly the meadow gives way to a willow thicket alive with warblers and goldfinches. Water seeps out of the ground into a miniature marsh. Springs dot the steep hillside all the way down to the geologically unique Rattlesnake Springs on the desert floor. Unaffected by drought, these springs come from fossil water trapped in a perched layer of water-saturated sediment.

Rattlesnake Springs, now closed to the public for recovery from years of overgrazing and a 250-square-mile brush fire in 2000, is a miniature canyon holding a free-flowing stream. Surrounded by dry desert, suddenly here is water. Peach willows have reestablished themselves after an ever-expanding elk herd was culled. From oil and gas drilling in the late 1950s, geologists know that the basalt layers here and on Saddle Mountain are more than ten thousand feet thick. In fact, test drills never reached the bottom of the basalt or found oil or gas.

The springs actually widen as we wander up the canyon. The water is thick with watercress. Larry, one of the group's leaders, gestures me over and asks me to kneel. Along the moist canyon walls, rusty steppe moss, *Tortula ruralis,* holds soil together. On our hands and knees we discover it is made of tiny starbursts. Trailing clematis vines drape through the trees as if we had entered a jungle. An owl flushes ahead, and, as if water itself created it, the willows are full of music—kinglets, sparrows, and wrens. We leave these wet, lush oases to their rightful inhabitants, grateful to know that out in the miserable heat of August, they have cool nooks for hiding. Besides, the Wanapum ancestral spirits crowd in on me, laughing gently at my tedious plant identification methods. They know all the names, the uses, and the stories automatically.

The Wanapum belong to this sacred mountains and spring. We are but fleeting visitors.

wallula gap and horse heaven hills

I slept near Wallula on a desert creek last night and awakened this morning to the gurgle of doves, wrens, quails, orioles, meadowlarks, ducks, and a snipe's winnowing wings. Someone is chortling down in the reeds like a turkey baster being squeezed under water. Last night I watched the Columbia River grow fat and sluggish again, writhing its way through a tangle of interstates, through Richland, through Kennewick, through Pasco, joining the Snake. Sergeant Ordway of Meriwether Lewis and William Clark's Corps of Discovery wrote of this confluence October 16, 1805, "the country around these forks is level smooth plain, no timber, not a tree to be seen as far as our eyes could extend." He also noted that "the river is remarkably clear and crowded with salmon in many places . . . great numbers of salmon dead on shore, floating on the water and on the bottom."

William Clark was impressed with the great number of Indians from many different tribes engaged in trade. He genuinely respected their culture. Of the Sokulk he wrote, "They ware short skirts and leather deer skin robes—live in happiness, take greater share in labor of woman, content to have one wife—have a mild disposition and temperament—not begging, and receive what is given with great joy." He also noted that the prickly pears were "the worst we have seen." The Lewis and Clark Museum at the confluence of the Snake and Columbia has enlarged photographs of the actual journal pages of the Corps of Discovery. As I stood copying them into my own journal, the men seemed to come alive and speak to me.

A lesser river must follow the landscape, but a great river has choices to make. Yakima and Rattlesnake ridges turned the Columbia eastward off its course to the Pacific. At Horse Heaven Hills it rebelled and sawed its way through. Just before the Wallula Gap carved from basalt in the Horse Heaven Hills, the Columbia turns west toward the sea.

From the road, I climb two-thirds of the way up the side of a three-hundred-foot pinnacle of the western Twin Sister. With a rope and a good belay I could stand on the very top, but a sign on private property asks us not to. The lava rock is jet black against the kelly green of the spring shrubs. In back of the pillars, pure white sand dunes are dusted with impressionistic wild flowers.

What a magnificent view! From here I can see high cliffs,

Two Sisters: Basalt towers near the Washington-Oregon border in the Wallula Gap

trains, the wide Columbia behind the McNary Dam, wheat fields in Oregon, and car wrecks rolled down Horse Heaven Hills. Steeply slanted light casts dramatic shadows, delineating layer after layer of buttes. Wind funnels up through the Wallula Gap until I cannot feel my hands, and my ears ring. Talus falls away below me in a near vertical angle of repose. The sky is stringent blue with mare's tails. White caps whip up on the river. A lone pelican, stark white and huge, with a bright orange bill and big yellow webbed feet, lands on the river and cocks his eye for a fish. Thousands of these white birds once fished this river.

The loss of a sense of abundance perhaps is the great tragedy of this age. I would love to have seen the Wallula Gap last century as a thousand-foot gorge with a wild river plunging through it. This once was a significant hunting and fishing place, due to its narrow opening in the basalt funneling game animals toward hunting blinds. Analysis of buffalo bone splinters indicated winter kills about four thousand years ago. Old stories still tell of Wallula Gap as a significant fishing site.

These two basalt pillars were once Cayuse Indian sisters. Coyote fell in love with three sisters who were building a salmon trap. The trickster watched them build by day, and at night would destroy their day's work. The sisters would rebuild each day, but Coyote would tear it down again each night. One morning, he found the three sisters crying and starving. He promised to build them a trap. He built the trap and they lived happily for many years. One day he became jealous of them and changed two sisters into basalt pillars and the third into a cave downriver. He himself became a rock to watch over them forever.

No doubt, Coyote is watching right now.

heat

August heat. As an experiment in pure desert, I drive up through Oregon toward Hanford Reach to experience the worst heat of summer. A hundred and thirteen degrees is not heat at all but a body of viscous polyethylene that coats one down into the lungs. The plants, which were so colorful and fruitful just two months ago, are dry, dormant rattles. Livestock are sweltering, miserable lumps. Birds silent. The heat is not heat but a sticky drapery, which hangs over me, over mouth and nose so I cannot breathe. I stay out in it purposefully, drink electrolytes and salts, but no food since morning. I grow weak, so dutifully force bits of tuna to my tongue and chew as if through gum erasers. Heat is not a temperature but a physical churning. Forty minutes later, I upchuck in the bitterbrush. In heat, logical thought does not work.

When I ate breakfast at the Rainbow Bar in Pendleton early this morning, I felt the warmth of community, of family, of continuity. Ten old cowboys sat smoking around Formica tables, shooting the breeze on the war, the economy, the heat, and how to achieve sex with a long-term partner. Colorful posters of dance-hall ladies and bucking broncos, and whirling beer signs, accompanied my eggs and bacon. In rural America, I always seek out these genuine, café-museums of vivid local history by driving slowly through downtown. Ninety years of framed photos, the grand winners of the Stampede Days rodeo since 1913, watched me eat breakfast in a dark wood booth. On my way to pay the bartender, I walked this line of large-hatted men back from the year 2002 curling around the two huge rooms of the bar. Something struck me at once: except for photographic printing technique, these images were remarkably similar. These fellows were cut of the same cloth, held the same values of family, bravery, and bronco riding. Last names repeated. First names ran to the manly and monosyllabic. The continuity struck me.

Now in the heat, north to Hanford.

What were once subtle, desert shades of beauty are sickly beige. Sky is pale blue gradating to dust storm gray on the horizon. The gold of cropped wheat fields glows far lighter than the gray sky. Tumbleweeds gather against fences until the entire structure is one immense, linear brush fire waiting for ignition. Cheat grass lines the highway in dirty gold. The highway crosses

Road in coulee bottom

a slack water, where once Chiawana frothed and thundered. Train tracks with yellow trains converge in the distance. The power grid flows out from the McNary Dam, towers so thick they look like English tweed—shimmering English tweed. Wide-open space, power, water, and big yellow trains: everything that suckles Hanford Nuclear Facility.

As I drive down out of the Horse Heaven Hills toward the Tri-Cities—Richland, Pasco, and Kennewick—there are no buildings. All is grayish brown lentil soup. Occasionally, rectangular lentils, cooked and stirred too long, pop out in the dust storm. I curve around through Pasco, then up through Richland, the nearby rattles of Rattlesnake Mountain barely visible in the soup. Rattlesnake Mountain itself is but a thin lavender outline in the lavender-gray soup. Haystacks stand in perfect cubism, molten gold toward the sun, and charcoal gray on their sides. New Russian thistle grows bright green and healthy. The equally invasive Russian olive blows silvery in the wind. In the draws, the alder are dying for lack of water. Nothing seems alive. The county's fire-dial sign reads FIRE DANGER EXTREME.

For those of us who never worked at Hanford, the nuclear facility is jarring for its lack of continuity. Family continuity, social fabric, town history, and ranching continuity. When the government seized the towns of White Bluff and Hanford, they seized people's stories about the land. Of course Hanford brought new stories.

War itself is the shattering of continuity. On an atomic level, nuclear fission is an ultimate lack of continuity. As I diverge from Highway 240 into the Department of Energy Hanford

Site, I am struck by the break between the outside world and the inside world. I drive north on a highway toward White Bluffs. Signs on fenced enclosures read NO ENTRANCE. The desert is so hot that a mirage turns the road to silver mirrors. White smoke rises from the mirrors, and a sign advises me to turn on my headlights.

No matter what reality exists within my small cab, it will soon dissolve for all those who travel in back of me into a haze of smoke and mirrors. A sign: "Area Three Hundred Clean Up Site." Ahead, a huge white dome rises, so organic in its perfect hemisphere as to imitate nature's seeds or bubbles. The bare-bone buildings are such flat squares in no colors that they disappear into desert neutrality.

Brutalism is an actual architectural style, meaning rough, untreated concrete, exaggerated structural features, unfinished materials, grandiose scale, exposed mechanical systems, and formalism. While most buildings on Hanford are practicality personified, several are significant high-style architecture. Buildings 337, 337B, and 331 in Battelle's Area 300 exhibit Brutalism. The Hanford Technical Library is art deco and Moderne style. Today a superheated wind is blowing so that buildings are melting in heat waves. Strict, straight lines, an extreme manifestation of the left-brain logic, are squirreling into rococo trim in the hot-air eddies.

I stop to write and have the sense I am being observed by security. I step out to stand in the heat for as long as I can.

One could die out here without buildings nearby. How utterly frail and boiled is this human shell. To mock me, a side-blotched lizard zaps up to my feet and does pushups to show me how large and ferocious he is. You win, I murmur.

My hair, so well adapted for warmth on northern wet, green isles, burns hot to the touch. My feet and lips feel swollen to four times their size. The rich, varied lithosols, which once fascinated me in their variety, vibrate beneath me, binding me to the ground like a prisoner to a medieval dungeon wall.

Wind comes, but not to cool. Rather it mimics a convection oven. My eyes dry out, catch airborne sand.

Heat is not a mere aspect of the desert: heat personifies the desert. Its howling cold in winter I can stand—with enough clothes. The first flocks of thousands of snow geese in February thrill me. The gush of spring wildflowers March through June is another essence of a desert. But which is the real essence?

Will the real desert please stand up?

Heat stands up. I stagger back and fall into the truck seat. A thunderstorm is rolling in over Rattlesnake Mountain. Afternoon, a blush of Pacific storm, a cyclone of moisture, whirs up through the Columbia Gorge. Cumulus clouds rapidly expand skyward becoming menacing gray cumulonimbus. Their five-mile-high tops flatten out into anvil shapes—high winds aloft.

The thunderheads, updrafts swelling them high into the atmosphere, develop a positive charge at their tops and a negative charge at bottom. Winds churn in convection cells, and ice crystals form at their tops. Earth is negatively charged, but due to the electrostatic repulsion of the negative cloud bottoms, a positive charge is induced and increases as the cloud strengthens. Positively charged ions push up to the top of high objects waiting

Charred remains of big sage

to establish a current to the cloud. A million volts per meter may build up, the air resistance is overcome, and instantly lightning strikes. Each path can carry over 200,000 amperes, heating to a million degrees the tree or aluminum chair of its affection.

Deep thunder, the mumbling voice of Zeus, grows louder, longer, and echoes over time (twenty seconds for one) and space (east to west over two hundred miles). Sounds like Scottish curling stones flipped end over end. I love such storms! Such storms bring danger: danger of being struck here on the flatlands, danger of setting the sagebrush on fire.

Yet such storms bring life. If there ever was a more apropos use of a masculine anger metaphor than for thunder's thick wave of sound, I can't think of it. An Old Testament God using lightning to strike fear and awe. Zeus rumbles and Athena springs from his head. Wisdom and nourishing rain. What did primitive man and woman feel with no twenty-first-century explanatory stories? For that original, primitive awe, I return to a time of a flash flood in Alaska when, unbeknownst to me, an ice dam broke far above in a glacier. Suddenly, with the noise of three locomotives, tan sludge five feet high roared down the dry riverbed toward my friend and me. We scrambled up the loose rubble of tossed, sliding river cobble just in time, then turned to watch as children watch. Incomprehension fused with thrill.

Gentle roars of wind and thunder announce the rain. As I run north for cover, out of the flat of Hanford, drops are explosive on my windshield, too fast for the wipers. Settling into a low hollow of willows, I consider other mighty roars of nature toward man or of man toward nature. The roar of the mile-high flood of broken Missoula Ice Dam waters sweeping at 65 miles per hour, carving out the Hanford landscape twelve thousand years ago. The roar of the Nagasaki bomb on August 9, 1945, as heard by a woman cyclist twenty miles away in the country. She watches as a tight ring-shaped cloud rushes toward her bike.

Two decades later, the grief-roar of a father downwind from the Green Run plutonium upon finding his third family member is suffering another form of cancer, this time leukemia. Those are the terrible roars. But this is a good roar, a roar of coliseums—roars that announce moisture, that celebrate the Coriolis effect of Earth's spinning storms. This storm's roar is beneficent.

The willows leap in unison to the direction of an unseen choreographer, Martha Graham, their arms bent in angst. Black cottonwood leaf clatter sounds just like a creek: sign of their water longing. The dark sky lights up, and I cringe in the thunder three seconds later. Crawling in the back of my truck under its canopy, I use a flashlight to read. The tall ridges all around beckon the thunder.

Up there on a ridge top, the Hindu god Krishna, in the opening scene of the Bhagavad Gita, readies Arjuna for battle by explaining to him why it is his duty to kill kith and kin. In his case, as in World War II, war embodied a higher duty. The dark karma of war and hope of reconstruction.

Lightning has long been the metaphor of spiritual illumination, the descent of power from heavenly wisdom to earth. Apollo's arrows represent sun rays and lightning, as well as the weapons of war. Krishna hurls the *varja,* the thunderbolt of both destruction and refertilization. The eagle on our own dollar bill holds lightning in one talon and peace in the other. The Tibetan *dorje,* a scepter, symbolizes thunder and masculine virility in balance with the bell, the symbol of feminine power and wisdom. Zeus's thundering anger and Athena springing from his splitting head, a symbol of wisdom. Nature's fire cycle clears downed woody debris, opening the forest floor for better habitat and healthier forests.

Two hours later, the storm disappears. Thirty-five degrees cooler, the desert air fills with volatile oils designed to protect desert plants from the sun. Nothing is more aromatic than this intense smell of desert after a rain. Sage, mint, saltbush, bitterbrush fill the nostrils with cleansing rosemary-like scents.

The air smells like hope itself.

The small dirt track straight up Saddle Mountain beckons. Now safe with no lightning, Saddle Mountain entices after a storm has broken. As I gain elevation, I can see for miles and miles. Scrims of clouds are pulling back across the west, revealing a pale, scrubbed sky. A triple rainbow arches in the east.

Under the soil, I can almost hear the rebirth of small roots. In a few hours, or tomorrow, tiny green sprouts will appear on certain desert plants adapted to take full advantage of the least moisture. Already, a lowly moss on the rocky mountaintop is expanding hopefully toward green.

At 1,790 feet, more than a quarter of a mile above the Columbia, I gaze one hundred miles north up Crab Creek and Channeled Scablands, the miniature Grand Canyon left by the Missoula floods. Abundant shallow lakes glint across the fields like silver coins—the Columbia Wildlife Refuge. In two days early one May, I counted 104 bird species there. Up from my willow ditch, I feel expansive on top of one great wrinkle in the earth's crust.

To the south the earth drops away in burnt-red and sage-green scallops down to the white Columbia River. The river shines brighter than the sky and the drenched landscape. Its crescent curves around the 59,000-acre Wahluke Unit, where I have spent many happy hours hiking in spring. Revealed to me for the first time, I discover the extensive Saddle Mountain wetland, essential for thousands of birds. No one is allowed in except for the occasional biologist.

South of the river, I can see all of Hanford Nuclear Reservation and feel a deep relief that its ability to blow up much of the world is being dismantled in an orderly fashion. Some claim that such weapons of mass destruction keep the peace, but as a naturalist-teacher-woman, I ain't buying it. Even if I had the wisdom to sort out the questions of war, my quiet voice would never be heard. Arjuna's army must march on forever in the Bhagavad Gita, but they only hold spears.

So far above the landscape, I straddle four empires like a Greek goddess—Crab Creek farmland, the Hanford Reservation, the distant blue Cascades, and the Tri-Cities urban sprawl glittering on the southeast skyline. The Fish and Wildlife Service banishes us humans—tires, t.p., fire rings, and all—from Saddle Mountain and the Wahluke from sunset until one hour before dawn. Alas, with the Hanford Reach so renewed and gleaming, I would like to play at being Athena just a little bit longer.

bibliography

Belnap, Jayne, Roger Rosentreter, Steve Leonard, Julie Hilty Kaltenecker, John Williams, and David Eldridge. *Biological Soil Crusts: Ecology and Management*. Technical Reference 1730-2. Denver, Colo.: U.S. Department of the Interior, Bureau of Land Management, National Science and Technology Center, 2001.

Clark, Lewis. *Field Guide to Wild Flowers of the Arid Flatlands in the Pacific Northwest*. Sidney, British Columbia: Gray's Publishing, 1975.

D'Antonio, Michael. *Atomic Harvest: Hanford and the Lethal Toll of America's Nuclear Arsenal*. New York: Crown Publishers, 1993.

Gerber, Michele Stenehjem. *On the Homefront: The Cold War Legacy of the Hanford Nuclear Site*. Lincoln: University of Nebraska Press, 1992.

Goin, Peter. *Nuclear Landscapes*. Baltimore: Johns Hopkins University Press, 1991.

Hanford Reach National Monument Web site.
http://hanfordreach.fws.gov/

Harvey, David. *History of the Hanford Site 1943–1990*. Richland, Wash.: Pacific Northwest National Laboratory, U.S. Department of Energy, 2001.

Hein, Teri. *Atomic Farmgirl: The Betrayal of Chief Qualchan, the Appaloosa, and Me.* Denver, Colo.: Fulcrum Publishing, 2000.

Hunn, Eugene. *Nch'i-Wána, "The Big River: Mid-Columbia Indians and Their Land."* Seattle: University of Washington Press, 1997.

Newsome, Heidi (United States Fish and Wildlife Service Field Ranger). Field lectures, Rattlesnake Mountain, Wash., May 2003.

Nisbet, Jack. Field lectures through the Whidbey Institute, The Hanford Reach, Wash., October 2002 and May 2003.

———. *Purple Flat Top: In Pursuit of a Place.* Seattle, Wash.: Sasquatch Books, 1996.

———. *Singing Grass, Burning Sage: Discovering Washington's Shrub-Steppe.* Portland, Oreg.: The Nature Conservancy, Graphic Arts Publishing, 2001.

———. *Sky People,* Mount Vernon, Wash.: Quartzite Books, 1984.

O'Connor, Georganne, and Karen Wieda. *Northwest Arid Lands: An Introduction to the Columbia Basin Shrub-Steppe.* Columbus, Ohio: Battelle Press, 2001.

Pacific Northwest National Laboratory Web site. http://www.pnl.gov/

Parish, Roberta, Ray Coupé, and Dennis Lloyd, eds. *Plants of Southern Interior British Columbia and the Inland Northwest.* Vancouver, British Columbia: Lone Pine Publishing, 1996.

Patterson, Paul (Senior Safety Analyst, Ares Corporation). Field lectures through the Whidbey Institute, The Hanford Reach, Wash., October 2002 and May 2003.

Relander, Click. *Drummers and Dreamers.* Seattle, Wash.: Northwest Interpretive Association, 1986.

Sackschewsky, Michael R., and Janelle L. Downs. *Vascular Plants of the Hanford Site.* Richland, Wash: Pacific Northwest National Laboratory, prepared for the U.S. Department of Energy, September 2001.

Sanger, S. L. *Hanford and the Bomb: An Oral History of World War II.* Seattle, Wash.: Living History Press, 1989.

Stapp, Darby C. Battelle's Pacific Northwest National Laboratory field lecture for the North Cascades Institute, The Hanford Reach, Wash., 2003.

Stapp, Darby C., and Michael S. Burney. *Tribal Cultural Resource Management: The Full Circle to Stewardship.* Heritage Resource Management Series, vol. 4. Walnut Creek, Calif.: AltaMira Press, 2002.

United States Department of Energy Hanford Site.
http://www.hanford.gov/

about the author

Susan Zwinger's award-winning first book, *Stalking the Ice Dragon* (University of Arizona Press, 1991), launched her career of natural history journeys, including *Still Wild, Always Wild*, *Women and Wilderness* (co-edited with Ann H. Zwinger), *The Last Wild Edge*, and numerous published essays. Combining her interest in the natural world with her talents as writer and artist, Zwinger's professional and volunteer experiences include National Park Service public information officer (on the Exxon oil spill), naturalist ranger, museum curator, and assistant professor. She now lives on an island off the coast of Washington, where she speaks with eagles and loons daily.

about the photographer

Skip Smith spent his first professional life as an entomologist. He was a professor of biology at Central Washington University, Ellensburg, Washington, for over 30 years. More than 25 years ago he developed his interest in photography and has worked in the arid regions of eastern Washington for several decades as both a biologist and a photographer. Smith has won several awards for his photography and is represented in several private and public collections.

Library of Congress Cataloging-in-Publication Data
Zwinger, Susan, 1947–
The Hanford Reach : a land of contrasts / text by Susan Zwinger ; photographs by Skip Smith.
p. cm. — (Desert places)
Includes bibliographical references.
ISBN 0-8165-2376-2 (pbk. : alk. paper)
1. Hanford Reach (Wash.)—Description and travel. 2. Hanford Reach (Wash.)—Pictorial works. 3. Natural history—Washington—Hanford Reach. 4. Desert ecology—Washington—Hanford Reach. 5. Steppe ecology—Washington—Hanford Reach. 6. Hanford Region (Wash.)—Description and travel. 7. Hanford Region (Wash.)—Pictorial works. 8. Columbia River Valley—Description and travel. 9. Columbia River Valley—Pictorial works. I. Smith, Stamford D. II. Title. III. Series.
F899.H36Z88 2004
917.97'5104—dc22
2004015054